CHECKERBOARD HOW-TO LIBRARY

COOL ART

Cool PAINTING

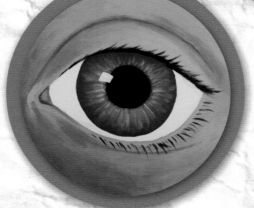

THE ART OF CREATIVITY FOR KIDS!

ANDERS HANSON

ABDO
Publishing Company

CONTENTS

Published by ABDO Publishing Company, 8000 West 78th Street, Edina, Minnesota 55439.

Copyright © 2009 by Abdo Consulting Group, Inc. International copyrights reserved in all countries.

No part of this book may be reproduced in any form without written permission from the publisher. The Checkerboard Library™ is a trademark and logo of ABDO Publishing Company.

Printed in the United States.

Editor: Pam Price

Series Concept: Nancy Tuminelly

Cover and Interior Design: Anders Hanson, Mighty Media

Photo Credits: Anders Hanson, Shutterstock

Library of Congress Cataloging-in-Publication Data
Hanson, Anders, 1980-
  Cool painting : the art of creativity for kids / Anders Hanson.
    p. cm. -- (Cool art)
  Includes index.
  ISBN 978-1-60453-143-5
1. Painting--Technique--Juvenile literature. I. Title.

ND1146.H35 2008
751.4--dc22

2008022243

Get the Picture!

When a step number in an activity has a colored circle around it, look for the picture that goes with it. The picture's border will be the same color as the circle.

2 ·············>

THE ART OF creativity

You Are Creative

Being creative is all about using your imagination to make new things. Coming up with new ideas and bringing them to life is part of being human. Everybody is creative! Creative thinking takes time and practice. But that's okay, because being creative is a lot of fun!

Calling All Artists

Maybe you believe that you aren't good at art. Maybe you have some skills that you want to improve. The purpose of this book is to help you develop your visual creativity. Remember that your artistic skills improve every time you make art. The activities in this book can help you become the creative artist you want to be!

Creativity Tips

- Stay positive.
- There is no wrong way to be creative.
- Allow yourself to make mistakes.
- Tracing isn't cheating.
- Practice, practice, practice.
- Be patient.
- Have fun!

Painting IS COOL!

*The only time I feel alive
is when I am painting.*
—Vincent Van Gogh

What Is Painting?

Painting is the act of putting paint on a surface. Paint is made of colored powder mixed with a sticky liquid. The colored powder is called pigment. It determines the color of the paint. The sticky liquid is called binder. It holds the pigment together.

Paints come in a broad range of colors. Color is a wonderful tool for expression because color affects the way people feel. With so many colors to choose from, artists can express a wide range of emotions within a painting.

PAINTING FROM A ROMAN
HOUSE (AD 1ST CENTURY)

STILL LIFE WITH BLUE TABLECLOTH (1909)
— HENRI MATISSE

From Artisan to Artist

Through the early centuries, culture, religion, and politics controlled what artists painted. Painters did not decide the subject matter, form, or imagery they painted. Painters were considered **artisans** rather than artists. Over time, however, painters became known as fine artists who painted what they wanted and signed their work.

The Power of Color

Painters use color to communicate feelings. They can also use it to make a painting look three-dimensional. Understanding how colors affect people will help you express yourself more clearly. Learning how to mix and combine colors effectively will help you make interesting, lifelike paintings.

Colors, like people, have personalities. Vincent van Gogh painted sunflowers for his visiting friend Paul Cézanne. Van Gogh used bright, warm yellows, oranges, and reds to welcome him and make him feel happy.

Everyone sees color differently. Color creates different feelings and opinions. Ask people what color something is or how a color makes them feel. You may be surprised by how different the answers are!

VASE WITH 12 SUNFLOWERS (1888)
—VINCENT VAN GOGH

Become a Painter!

Learning to paint is fun because all you need is paint, something to paint on, and something to paint with. There is no right or wrong way to paint. You can plan, or you can be **spontaneous**. It is up to you to determine what will work best for you.

If you are not satisfied with your first paintings, remember this. It takes practice to become a good painter. You don't need to be good at art now to become a great artist. You just need the desire to learn, experiment, and become better!

Don't Be a Judge!

When discussing a painting, avoid using the words listed below. They offer judgments without saying much about the character of the work. Instead, look at how the artist used composition and **techniques**. Try to understand what the artist was trying to achieve. See pages 8 through 15 to read about these elements.

- good
- bad
- right
- wrong
- silly
- stupid

TOOLS OF THE TRADE

PALETTE

RED ACRYLIC

CRAYONS

YELLOW ACRYLIC

BLUE ACRYLIC

GREEN ACRYLIC

WHITE ACRYLIC

BLACK ACRYLIC

FLAT BRUSHES

ROUND BRUSHES

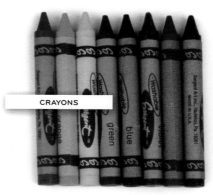

Each activity in this book has a list of the tools and materials you will need. When you come across a tool you don't know, turn back to these pages. You can find most of these items at your local art store.

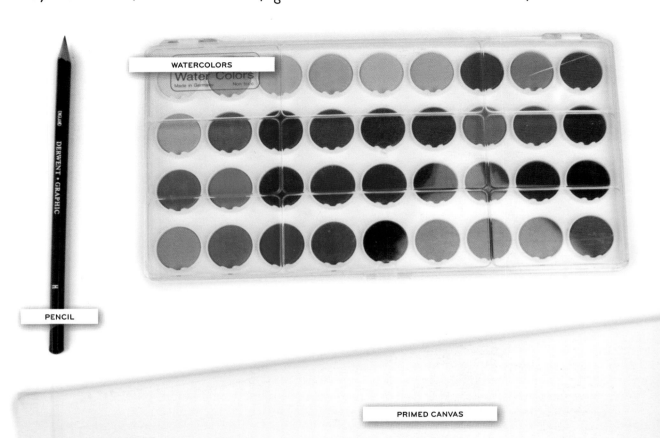

PENCIL

WATERCOLORS

Water Colors
Made in Germany   Non toxic

PRIMED CANVAS

WATERCOLOR PAPER

Basic Elements

These are the elements that make up images. All paintings can be described by these key **concepts**.

Point

The point is the most basic element of painting. Touching a painting tool to a surface and immediately removing it creates a point.

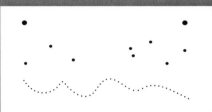

Line

Connecting two points creates a line. Lines can be straight, angled, or curved. They may be thick or thin. Lines can be hard and rigid or soft and sketchy.

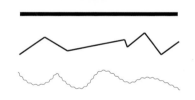

Shape

When lines enclose a space, they create a shape. A shape can be **geometric**, such as a circle or a square, or **irregular**. Shapes may be empty or solid.

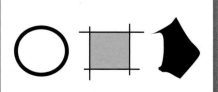

Pattern

Points, lines, and shapes can create a pattern when they repeat in an organized and **predictable** way.

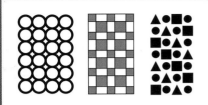

Texture

You can create texture by repeating points, lines, or shapes. Make them so small that you can't easily see the individual elements.

Value

Value describes how light or dark a color is. Light objects have little value. Dark objects have a lot of value.

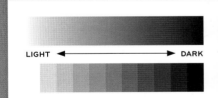

LIGHT ◄──────► DARK

Color

You can make every color by mixing the primary colors. Mixing any two primary colors creates a secondary color. See page 14 for more about color.

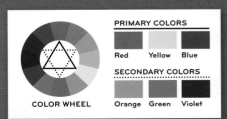

COLOR WHEEL

PRIMARY COLORS
Red   Yellow   Blue

SECONDARY COLORS
Orange   Green   Violet

Composition

Bringing together the basic elements to make a work of art is called composition. The following ideas will help you create great compositions!

Focal Point

The focal point is the first thing you see when you look at a painting. Without a focal point, a painting may seem **chaotic**.

FOCUSED

UNFOCUSED

Balance

Balance refers to the arrangement of elements in a painting. Evenly spread objects create balance. Objects grouped in one area create an unbalanced composition.

BALANCED

UNBALANCED

Movement

Movement occurs when things appear to be traveling across a painting. The image on the left moves like a river. The one on the right feels calm, like a lake.

MOVEMENT

STILLNESS

Space

Whenever lines enclose a space, two shapes are made. The shape inside the lines is called positive space. The shape outside the lines is called negative space. When these shapes work well together, the composition is more interesting.

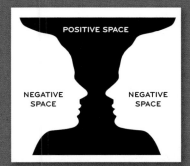

POSITIVE SPACE

NEGATIVE SPACE

NEGATIVE SPACE

Rhythm

Rhythm isn't just for musicians! Artists repeat brushstrokes or shapes to give their work rhythm.

RHYTHMIC LINES

Harmony

When two or more elements in a painting share **characteristics**, they are in **harmony**. When elements don't have much in common, they are **dissonant**. Characteristics that help create harmony include color, size, and shape.

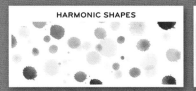

HARMONIC SHAPES

DISSONANT SHAPES

Contrast

Contrast occurs when a work has both extremes of an element. Using smooth and rough textures, light and dark values, and large and small shapes are ways to add contrast.

LOW VALUE CONTRAST

HIGH VALUE CONTRAST

Techniques

Artists use various **techniques** to create the elements of a painting. Pick up a brush and try these techniques as you read about them.

Using a Brush

There are many types and sizes of brushes. Use small round brushes for painting details. Use large flat brushes to quickly paint big spaces. Always wash a brush with warm water after you're done using it, or before changing colors.

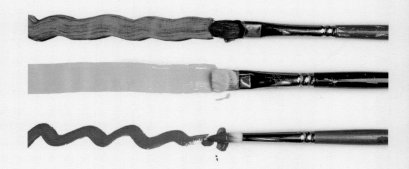

Underpainting

Paintings are often made in layers. Layering coats of paint creates subtle changes in tone as well as richer colors. The first layer of color in a painting is called the underpainting. It acts as a foundation for the layers painted on top of it.

UNDERPAINTING

FINISHED PAINTING

Glazing

Glazing is one way to layer paint over the underpainting. To make a glaze, mix a little water into paint. Apply the thinned paint over a dry underpainting. Because the glaze is thin, some of the underpainting will still be visible.

GREEN GLAZE ON WHITE

GREEN GLAZE ON RED

GREEN DRY BRUSH ON WHITE

GREEN DRY BRUSH ON RED

Dry Brushing

To dry brush, gently wipe some paint from the brush before applying it to the painting. The dry brush will leave rough, textured strokes. Because dry brushing makes thin, scattered marks, the paint beneath will show through.

Wet-on-Wet

Applying wet paint to an area that is already wet is called wet-on-wet. Wet-on-wet is a fun and unpredictable technique. You never know exactly how the washes will mix with each other or bleed into surrounding areas. So, it's nearly impossible to control the results!

Color Theory

Learning how colors relate to each other will help you create more interesting paintings!

Primary Colors

The primary colors are red, yellow, and blue. All of the other colors can be made by mixing different amounts of primary colors together. Primary colors cannot be made from other colors.

Secondary Colors

Mixing two primary colors together creates a secondary color. The secondary colors are orange, green, and purple.

red + yellow = orange

yellow + blue = green

blue + red = purple

The Color Wheel

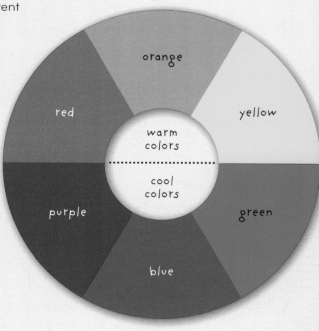

orange

red

yellow

warm colors

cool colors

purple

green

blue

Tints and Shades

Adding white to a color creates a tint. Adding black to a color creates a shade. Study the chart on the left. Each circle is a pure color that does not have black or white added to it. The colored bar above each circle shows that color's tints. The colored bar below each circle shows a range of that color's shades.

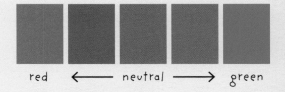

red ← neutral → green

Complementary Colors

Every color has a complementary color. When you look at a color wheel, complementary colors are opposite each other. Red and green are on opposite sides of the color wheel, so they are complementary colors. Blue's complement is orange. Purple and yellow are also complementary colors. Placing complementary colors next to each other makes both colors seem more vibrant.

Colorfulness

Mixing equal amounts of complementary colors creates a neutral, or gray, color. If you add a little green to red, you get a muddy, grayish red. Adding a little red to green makes the green more neutral and less colorful. This works for all complementary colors.

PAINTED MUSIC

Paint a feeling with primary colors!

Stuff You'll Need

Music, three brushes, palette or paper plate, acrylic paints (primary colors only), cup of water, watercolor paper or canvas

Setting Up

- Cover your workspace with newspaper, paper towels, or cardboard. The paper will catch drips and splatters.

- Give yourself enough space to work.

- Place your painting tools within arm's reach.

- Work in a well-lit area.

- Use a plastic cup filled with water for rinsing brushes. You can dry wet brushes with extra paper towels.

1   Choose some music to listen to while you paint. It can be any kind of music you want.

2   Set up three brushes, the three primary colors of acrylic paint, a cup of water, and the canvas.

3   Turn on the music and start painting! Use colors, lines, and shapes to express how the music makes you feel.

4   After you are done, notice the colors you used. What kinds of shapes and marks did you make? Can you see any patterns in your painting that match the beat of the music?

Are You Feeling Blue?

In art, you can use color to express how you feel. Look at the bluish painting on the right. Now look at the orange painting on the opposite page. Think of a couple of words that describe how each painting makes you feel.

Warm colors, such as red, orange, and yellow, tend to make people excited or happy. Cool colors, such as purple, blue, and green, can make people feel relaxed or sad. Now you know why people sometimes say they are feeling blue when they feel sad!

5   Now make a new painting while listening to different music. Compare your paintings and see how the colors and shapes changed.

MONOCHROME MONSTER

Mix tints and shades of blue to create a super sea serpent!

Stuff You'll Need

Pencil, watercolor paper or canvas, palette or paper plate, acrylic paints, brushes

1. Ancient sailors told stories of giant monsters that lived in the sea. Try to picture what a sea monster might look like. Using a pencil, draw your monster so that it covers most of your paper. If you like, draw some clouds behind it.

2. Draw a line where the sky meets the sea. It shouldn't overlap any parts of your monster. This is because the monster is in the foreground and blocks the view of anything directly behind it.

3. Put some white and some blue acrylic paints on a palette or a paper plate. Mix blue into white until you have a light-blue tint. Paint the sky this color. Leave the clouds, the sea, and the monster unpainted.

4. Add some more blue paint to your palette. Paint your monster's skin this solid blue.

5. Now paint the water at the bottom of your paper the same solid blue. Use wavy, choppy strokes to represent the texture of seawater. As you work your way up toward the horizon line, occasionally mix small amounts of black into the blue. By the time you've reached the horizon line, you should be painting with a dark-blue shade.

6. Paint your monster's eyes, nose, and mouth with tints and shades of blue.

A SEA OF COLOR

Create a beautiful water world with complementary colors!

Stuff You'll Need

Crayons, watercolor paper, watercolors, brushes

1. Get out some watercolor paper and crayons. Draw several fish with an orange crayon. You can draw them all the same size and shape. Or they can all be different. If you need help drawing fish, look at the ones in the example. You can also look through nature magazines for pictures of fish.

2. With a blue crayon, draw some tall wavy shapes that look like seaweed. They should look like they're behind the fish. So don't draw these shapes on top of the fish.

3. Paint all around the fish with blue watercolor. You'll notice that something interesting happens when you paint over the crayon lines of the seaweed. The crayon wax repels the paint! Let the watercolor dry.

4. Paint another layer of blue watercolor over the seaweed. This will make it a bit darker than the surrounding water.

5. Orange and blue are on opposite sides of the color wheel. That means they're complementary colors. Paint your fish with orange watercolors. Notice how complementary colors seem much more vivid when they appear side by side.

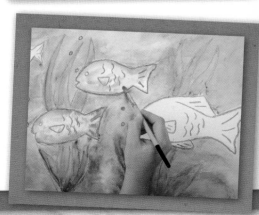

LOONY LANDSCAPE

Mix secondary colors to create a crazy, colorful landscape!

Stuff You'll Need

Pencil, canvas or watercolor paper, palette or paper plate, acrylic paint, brushes

1 Find a picture of a landscape that you would like to paint. Or, better yet, paint what you can see from your window or backyard.

2 Using a pencil, lightly sketch the outline of your landscape. Don't worry about any details. You'll soon paint over this drawing.

3 Put some red, blue, and yellow paint on a paper plate or a palette. Mix pairs of primary colors to create secondary colors. See pages 14–15 if you're not sure how to mix secondary colors. Try mixing different amounts of primary colors to create different tones of the secondary colors.

4 Now paint your landscape using only the secondary colors. This means that you'll paint with colors that are different from how things really appear! Your grass doesn't have to be green. You can make it purple or orange!

5 Use different sizes and shapes of brushes. See what different kinds of brush strokes you can make. Strong brush marks can make interesting textures. Many brush strokes going in the same direction can create a sense of motion.

WARM AND COOL

Use the natural values of colors to create a cool still life!

Stuff You'll Need
Still life arrangement, watercolor paper, pencil, watercolors, brush

1. A still life is an arrangement of objects. Find three or four simple objects that look like they'd be fun to paint. Arrange them close together on a table.

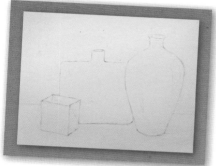

2. You need a strong source of light for this project. If your arrangement isn't getting a lot of light, you'll need a lamp. Ask an adult to help you set up a lamp close by.

3. Start by drawing a light sketch with a pencil. The objects should fill up most of the paper.

4. Look for the light areas, or highlights, of the objects. You will leave the lightest areas unpainted. These areas are usually small reflections on shiny or smooth objects.

5. Now paint the objects using only the warm colors, which are yellow, orange, and red. Start with the light colors. Paint the second-lightest areas with yellow paint. Orange is a little darker than yellow, so use it on the slightly darker areas. Allow the colors to blend using wet-on-wet **technique**.

6. Now find the dark areas, or shadows, of the objects. As you begin to paint these areas, use red paint. Use wet-on-wet technique and allow the colors to mix on the paper.

7. Your objects should now look somewhat three-dimensional. The goal is to create the illusion of form without using black or white.

8 Now paint the background using only the cool colors, which are green, blue, and purple.

9 Start with the lightest color, green. Then move on to the darker colors, blue and purple. Begin by painting the lightest areas of the table green.

10 While the green is still wet, paint the medium-valued areas blue. Then paint the shadows on the table purple.

11 Don't worry about painting all the details in the background. You can just paint it a solid color if you like. Try to make all the strokes go in one direction. The example has a blue background.

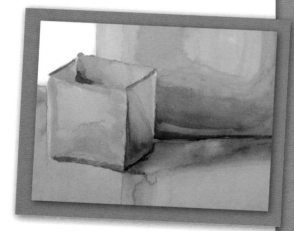

Warm Up or Cool Down?

People tend to notice warm colors before cool colors. Warm colors seem to come forward, and cool colors seem to move back. Look at the image below and compare it with the finished painting from the exercise. Which colors do you look at first? Notice that the objects in the painting from the exercise draw your eye more than the objects in this painting do.

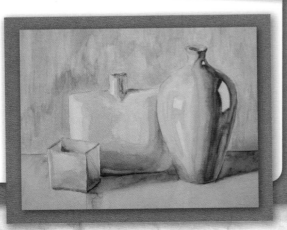

THE ARTIST'S EYE

Realistically paint one of your most interesting features!

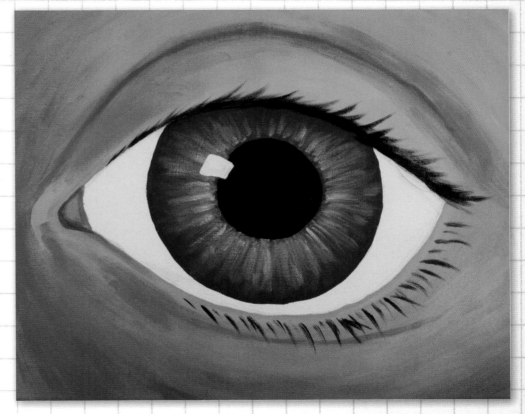

Stuff You'll Need

Mirror, pencil, canvas or watercolor paper, palette or paper plate, acrylic paints, brushes

1. Take a close look at one of your eyes in a mirror. Notice that the basic shape of your eye looks more like an almond than a circle. With a pencil, lightly sketch the outline of one eye on your canvas. Draw it large.

2. The inside part of your eye is made with two circles. The large colored circle is called the iris. The eyelids often cover the top and bottom of the iris. Inside the iris is a small black circle called the pupil. Draw these two circles.

3. The inside corner of the eye is a small pink area. Draw this area and any other **contours** you can see around your eye. Add a curved line to mark the crease in the upper eyelid.

4. Get out your acrylic paints and a paper plate or a palette. Try to mix a color that matches your skin tone. For lighter skin tones, mix white and yellow with a little red and a tiny bit of blue. For darker skin tones, mix white and brown with some red. Paint the area around the eye with skin-colored paint.

5. Try to mix a color that matches your eye color. Paint the iris with this color. Mix red and white to make pink. Paint the inner corner pink. Finally, paint the pupil black.

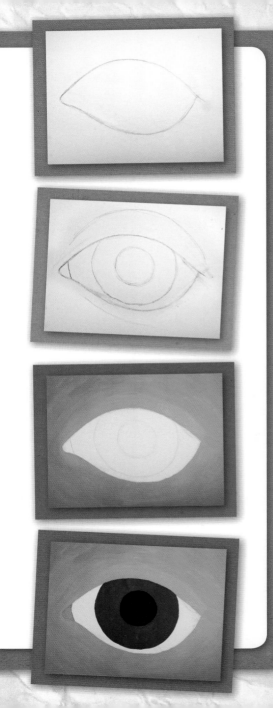

28

6 Mix your skin color again. Then lighten it by adding more white paint. Look for the light areas, or highlights, of the skin around your eye. Paint these areas with the lighter skin-colored paint.

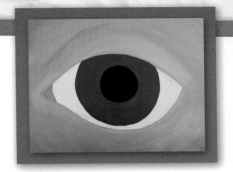

7 Mix another batch of skin-colored paint. But this time, don't add quite as much white as in the first batch. You'll end up with a slightly darker skin-colored paint. Find the dark areas, or shadows, of the skin around your eye. Paint these areas with the color you just mixed.

8 The inner part of the iris is usually lighter than the rest. Dry brush white paint over the inner part of the iris. Each stroke should start by the pupil and finish near the outer edge of the iris.

9 The surface of your eye is smooth, like a mirror. It's so smooth that you can see things reflected in it. Bright light from windows or lamps can create white areas on the iris or the pupil. Look for any shapes of reflected light and paint them white.

10 Paint another coat of black over the pupil. Avoid any highlights you added in the last step. Add your eyelashes with black paint. Notice that they don't go straight up or down. The upper eyelashes are thicker and closer together than the bottom ones. Finally, add some red paint to the edges of the inner corner of the eye (see the finished painting on page 27).

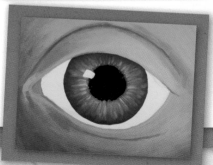

what's next?

Taking Care of Your Paintings

If you're not going to hang a painting, make sure you store it properly. That way, you can show people how you got your start when you become famous!

- If you have large, loose watercolor papers, consider buying an inexpensive cardboard portfolio to keep them in. You can find one at any art store. And, cardboard portfolios actually work better than the expensive leather portfolios!

- Put a sheet of newsprint or an extra sheet of paper between paintings in your portfolio. This will prevent them from rubbing off on one another.

- Canvases are even easier to take care of. Just wrap them in paper and store them in a dark area.

Try Something New!

The activities in this book are just a few examples of fun painting projects you can do. Once you've completed them all, go back and try some of the projects with different materials or subjects. Then make up some projects of your own!

Other Types of Paint

The projects in this book use watercolor and acrylic paints. That's because they dry fast and they're easy to clean up. But there are other types of paint to choose from.

- alkyd
- casein
- encaustic, or hot wax
- gouache
- oil
- tempera

GLOSSARY

artisan – a skilled person who earns a living by practicing a craft or a trade.

characteristic – a quality or a feature of something.

chaotic – of or relating to a state of total confusion.

concept – an idea.

contour – the outline of a shape, especially a curving or an irregular shape.

dissonant – having parts that don't go well together.

geometric – made up of straight lines, circles, and other simple shapes.

harmony – having parts that go well together.

irregular – lacking symmetry or evenness.

monochrome – having only one color.

predictable – being able to guess the outcome of an event based on reason, experience, or observation.

spontaneous – based on instinct or natural feeling.

technique – a method or style in which something is done.

Web Sites

To learn more about cool art, visit ABDO Publishing Company on the World Wide Web at **www.abdopublishing.com**. Web sites about cool art are featured on our Book Links page. These links are routinely monitored and updated to provide the most current information available.

INDEX